The Fall of Constantinople: The Rise of the Ottoman Empire and the End of the Byzantine Empire

By Charles River Editors

15th century depiction of the Ottoman siege.

About Charles River Editors

Charles River Editors provides superior editing and original writing services across the digital publishing industry, with the expertise to create digital content for publishers across a vast range of subject matter. In addition to providing original digital content for third party publishers, we also republish civilization's greatest literary works, bringing them to new generations of readers via ebooks.

Sign up here to receive updates about free books as we publish them, and visit Our Kindle Author Page to browse today's free promotions and our most recently published Kindle titles.

Introduction

A picture of the fall of Constantinople by Theophilos Hatzimihail

The Fall of Constantinople (1453)

In terms of geopolitics, perhaps the most seminal event of the Middle Ages was the successful Ottoman siege of Constantinople in 1453. The city had been an imperial capital as far back as the 4th century, when Constantine the Great shifted the power center of the Roman Empire there, effectively establishing two almost equally powerful halves of antiquity's greatest empire. Constantinople would continue to serve as the capital of the Byzantine Empire even after the Western half of the Roman Empire collapsed in the late 5th century. Naturally, the Ottoman Empire would also use Constantinople as the capital of its empire after their conquest effectively ended the Byzantine Empire, and thanks to its strategic location, it has been a trading center for years and remains one today under the Turkish name of Istanbul.

The end of the Byzantine Empire had a profound effect not only on the Middle East but Europe as well. Constantinople had played a crucial part in the Crusades, and the fall of the Byzantines meant that the Ottomans now shared a border with Europe. The Islamic empire was viewed as a threat by the predominantly Christian continent to their west, and it took little time for different European nations to start clashing with the powerful Turks. In fact, the Ottomans would clash with Russians, Austrians, Venetians, Polish, and more before collapsing as a result of World War

I, when they were part of the Central powers.

The Ottoman conquest of Constantinople also played a decisive role in fostering the Renaissance in Western Europe. The Byzantine Empire's influence had helped ensure that it was the custodian of various ancient texts, most notably from the ancient Greeks, and when Constantinople fell, Byzantine refugees flocked west to seek refuge in Europe. Those refugees brought books that helped spark an interest in antiquity that fueled the Italian Renaissance and essentially put an end to the Middle Ages altogether.

The Fall of Constantinople traces the history of the formation of the Ottoman Empire, the siege that toppled the city, and the dissolution of the Byzantine Empire. Along with pictures depicting important people, places, and events, you will learn about the fall of Constantinople like never before, in no time at all.

The Fall of Constantinople: The Rise of the Ottoman Empire and the End of the Byzantine Empire

About Charles River Editors

Chapter 1: Islam and the Birth of the Ottoman Empire

In contrast to Christianity, where the emphasis of the religion lies in the salvation of individual souls, in Islam, the goal is the construction of a perfect, universal Islamic community. The word khalifate, or "one and only," conjures for the Islamic world the same word that "empire" does for the world of Western Europe. By definition, there can only be one true khalifate.

However, by the 10th century, the word had come to mean in practice something more like "secular empire." The Islamic world was divided into three khalifates: the Fatimid Khalifate (covering Egypt and northern Africa), the Abbasid Khalifate (covering most of the present-day Middle East and southwest central Asia), and the Umayyad Khalifate (centered in Andalusia). The Abbasid Khalifate entered the 11th century with the most territory and the richest kingdom, but their grand size also proved to be a weakening force. Just as Rome grew too big for one ruler to command its entire jurisdiction, so did the Abbasid khalifate. The Abbasids had to create a vast bureaucracy to administer their empire, and the khalifa disappeared behind his own machinery to the point of becoming invisible to his subjects.

Exacerbating this problem was the use of mamluks. The word mamluks means slaves, and in this case, the word specifically referred to young male Turks conscripted to act as the corps of bodyguards for the khalifa. At this point in time, "Turks" did not refer to people living in Turkey but rather to the ethnic group, which originated on the steppes of Central Asia. In time, the majority of Turks would be Muslim, but at this point in time, the mamluks were brought into the khalifa as children, raised as Muslims in special schools, and taught martial skills. This was deemed necessary because Turks had a reputation to be uncivilized and pugnacious, but the mamluks only proved more uncontrollable once they were educated. The young bodyguards were so arrogant and violent that they played a role in making the khalifa unpopular with his constituents and even seem foreign to them.

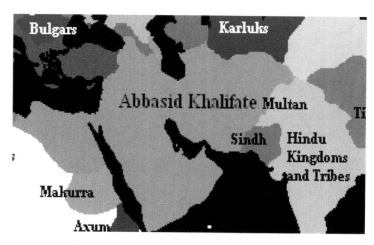

The Abbasid khalifate in the 11th century

On top of the internal challenge of keeping the mamluks under control, the empire was constantly fighting the encroachment of Turkish nomads from outside to keep them from crossing into their civilized world and wreaking havoc. Eventually, however, the Turks became too strong to suppress, both inside and outside the khalifate, and in some places, mamluks killed their masters and founded their own dynasties. Other Turks crossing in from outside ruined cities, plundered them, and laid waste to crops. The highways became unsafe, banditry became common, trade declined, and poverty spread. With Turks in power, there was a great deal of anxiety in the Islamic world.

Troubles increased with two new and powerful foreign groups that threatened the khalifate as well: the Franj (Crusaders) and the Mongols. In 1095, Pope Urban II ordered the first Crusade, sending Christian soldiers to the Holy Land with the mission of expelling the Turks from Jerusalem. In fact, the Crusaders took these instructions to its bloodiest extent, bringing extreme carnage to every city in their path, until their damage was stopped by a series of strong Muslim leaders. The first was the Turkish general Zangi, who began as governor of Mosul, then took Aleppo and gradually absorbed other cities until he could rightly be called the king of a united Syria. Zangi was loved by his soldiers because he lived as ruggedly as his soldiers, but more importantly to his success as a leader, he eliminated flatterers from his court and built a network of informers throughout Syria that kept his governors in line. Then, in 1144, Zangi conquered Edessa, marking the first sizable city that the Muslims had taken back from the crusaders. With the recapture of Edessa, one of the four "Crusader Kingdoms" ceased to exist. The fear that spread in Europe as a result of Zangi's triumph sparked the organization of a second crusade, which turned out to be ineffectual.

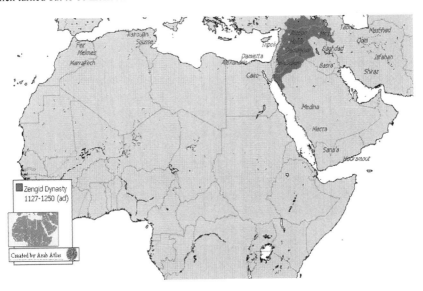

Zangi's empire

Zangi believed in the power of jihad as an instrument for unifying Muslims. The term jihad had only come into usage again after the Crusaders' carnage at Jerusalem, when several jurists began delivering sermons that used the word in an effort to provoke Muslim resistance by categorizing the invasion as a holy war. However, because the word had fallen out of use centuries earlier (the rapid expansion of Islam meant that the majority of Muslims lived far from the frontier line, and far from any enemy of Islam), it did not catch on at first. Adding to the challenge of arousing Muslim energies to jihad was the fact that Zangi, foul-mouthed and hard-drinking, offended many of the ulama (scholars of the Koran). Nonetheless, he set the stage for a succession of rulers that successfully defended the Muslim world until Europe's crusading impulse died off at the start of the 13th century.

Ultimately, the damage caused by the Crusades paled in comparison to the next assault on the Islamic empire, made by the Mongols. At the end of the 14th century, Timur-i-lang (also anglicized as Tamerlane), an even more bloodthirsty descendant of Genghis Khan, ravaged the Muslim world. The historian Ibn al-Athir called the onslaught "a tremendous disaster" the likes of which the world will never experience again "from now until its end." But most importantly, the carnage left the Muslim world considering their ambitions for a perfect, unified Islamic society and wondering what went wrong. The most vigorous response came from the Syrian jurist Ibn Taymiyah, who asserted there was nothing wrong with Islam - its validity was not being challenged by these wars - but that the problem lay with Muslims who had stopped practicing true Islam. God had therefore punished them by making them weak, and in order to become victorious again, Muslims needed to practice a purer, more adherent form of the religion by purging Islam of all new ideas, interpretations, and innovations.

Taymiyah also proposed that jihad was a core obligation of every Muslim, and he meant jihad in the most literal sense, calling every Muslim to violence. Taymiyah even went to battle against the Mongols himself. Taymiyah's name for the fundamentalist doctrine that he proposed was Salafism, whose long form means "the pious (or pristine) originals." Though he only built up a moderate following, he was an avid pamphleteer and propagandist, and he is partially responsible for building up the interest in jihad in the Muslim world.

Another response to the cultural breakdown that followed the Crusades and the Mongol terrors was the proliferation of Sufism, a broad-minded and undogmatic interpretation of Islam that can be understood as the exact opposite of Taymiyah's philosophy. Sufism is a type of Islamic mysticism that shares some ideas with Buddhism and Hindu mysticism, and Sufis are individuals who are dissatisfied with the bureaucratization of religion and turn inward, looking for a personal mystical union with God. Sufis shared a common goal but had varied ideas about how to achieve their mystical unions, so when a Sufi seemed to break through, he became a magnet for other seekers. "Sufi brotherhoods" thus formed around prominent individual Sufis, and these seekers lived, worked, and practiced their religion together under the guidance of their sheikh ("old man").

Since Islam's goal is the construction of a perfect community rather than individual union with God, Sufi brotherhoods operated less as monastic orders, where each monk is focused on his own asceticism, and more as chivalric orders. Those brotherhoods, which evolved to become something closer to bands of mystical knights, espoused an ethos called *futuwwah*, whose meaning is similar to the European code of knightly valor, courtly love, and chivalric honor. They illustrated these ideals through mythological and poetic anecdotes about early Muslim heroes.

Sufi orders proliferated throughout the Muslim world, but most numerously and consequently in Asia Minor, also known as Anatolia (present-day Turkey). Asia Minor had long been the battlefield dividing Turkish Muslims and European Christians, but since the Crusades had come to an end, Turkish princes more or less were in control of the eastern portion of Asia Minor, and the Byzantine Empire more or less controlled the western parts. Furthermore, the Mongol massacres had driven fresh groups of Turkish nomads out of Central Asia and into Asia Minor. As a result, Sufi orders flourished in this environment because they provided the protection, aid, and community services that the lawless region lacked. In Asia Minor, Sufi orders collaborated with merchants' and artisans' guilds called *akhi* (the Turkish word for *futuwwah*), whose purpose was similar to unions: protecting ordinary people from the uncertainties of the time. The orders intertwined with everyone, from the peasantry to the aristocratic military groups.

Eventually, the Sufi brotherhoods most devoted to futuwwah ideals developed into *ghazi* ("warrior saint") corporations. Almost like Christian military orders, except without a central figure to ordain them, the Ghazis adopted special headgear and cloaks, had initiation rituals and vows, and centered their lives around campaigns into Christian territory. Hundreds of Ghazis of all sizes sprung up in Asia Minor, and slowly they marched toward the hazy line of Byzantine territory. Eventually, the Ghazi knights were going toe-to-toe with Constantinople.

Depiction of Ottoman Ghazis in battle.

While the history of the region is fairly well-established, the exact beginning of the Ottoman Empire is shrouded in mystery and legend. It is traditionally dated to 1299 CE for the reason that it corresponds to the year 699 in the Islamic calendar; in a rare coincidence, the centuries turned at the same time for both cultures. At the time, the Ottomans were just one of many Islamic Turkish groups in Anatolia, but under their founder and leader, Osman, they proved to be the most effective and powerful of the myriad brotherhoods. It's believed that Osman was born of simple origins in northwest Anatolia to a tribal chief named Ertugrul, and the Ottoman Empire's founding myth states that Osman dreamed of his future power one night while sleeping in the house of a holy man. Caroline Finkel quotes in her book, *Osman's Dream*, "He saw that a moon arose from the holy man's breast and came to sink in his own breast. A tree then sprouted from his navel and its shade compassed the world. Beneath this shade tree there were mountains, and streams flowed forth from the foot of each mountain. Some people drank from these running waters, others watered gardens, while yet others caused fountains to flow. When Osman awoke he told the story to the holy man, who said, 'Osman, my son, congratulations, for God has given the imperial office to you and your descendants and my daughter Malhun shall be your wife.'" Though this story was communicated well after Osman's death, it became one of the world's most resilient myths of the founding of an empire.

Medieval depiction of Osman

1301 marks the first military encounter between Osman and the Byzantine Empire, when the Battle of Bapheus took place near the Sea of Marmara, but it would be many years before the Ottomans could truly challenge the Byzantines for power. That said, compared with other Islamic tribes in Anatolia, the Ottomans started with a geographical advantage by being located near Constantinople from the start, and they conquered several villages in the vicinity of the city early on. When Osman passed away in 1323 or 1324, he had secured the majority of northwest Anatolia for his heirs, and his son Orhan took over the leadership of the Ottomans. One of Orhan's first successes was to capture the city of Iznik, after a years-long siege, and the length that the Ottomans persisted in their sieges testifies to their manpower and tenacity.

Chapter 2: The Byzantine Empire Before the Fall

If the fall of Constantinople marked the end of the Byzantine Empire, it was only the apex of a long, slow decline. One place to start tracing the story of that decline is all the way back in 1341, when Emperor Andronicus III Palaeologus died and left no instructions regarding his successor. After strife between many parties, Andronicus's chief adviser, John Cantacuzenus, who had the support of the army, was crowned. Even from that moment, John Cantacuzenus understood that his empire needed help on a large scale, so in the first weeks of 1345, he made contact with the Ottoman Sultan Orhan. The two became friendly - at least on the surface - and Orhan even fell in love with John Cantacuzenus' daughter Theodora. Those two were married in 1346.

Medieval depiction of Andronicus III Palaeologus

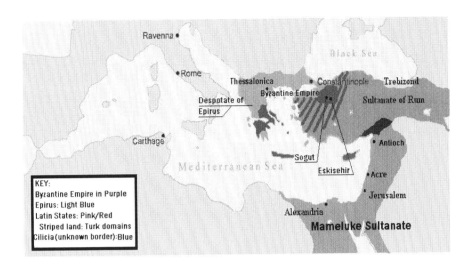

Map of the region during Andronicus III's reign.

John Cantacuzenus depicted as an emperor and a monk.

Western depiction of Sultan Orhan

On Easter Sunday of 1346, Stephen Dushan was crowned by the Serbian archbishop as the emperor of the Serbs and Greeks. He entered Constantinople with 1,000 men and emerged six days later, victorious in forging an agreement with John Cantacuzenus that the two men would be co-emperors. It is possible that John Cantacuzenus could have prevented the decline of the empire had he acted decisively when he first came to power, but by 1347, the problems of division and bankruptcy had compounded and Stephen Dushan was in the mix. Stephen Dushan posed a large problem because his empire was larger than the Byzantine Empire and he coveted Constantinople because his own country, Serbia, was landlocked.

Political problems had to be set aside, however, when the Black Death hit the region in 1347 and killed nearly 90% of the population. By the end of the plague's terrors, the empire was limited to Thrace and a few Aegean Islands. John Cantacuzenus attempted to consolidate his power by putting his sons in charge of certain parts of the territory, but more troubles came. Andronicus III Palaeologus' son, John V Palaeologus, had formed an alliance with the Venetians and was so successful in fighting the Byzantines that in 1347 he was crowned co-emperor. John Cantacuzenus tried unsuccessfully to depose John V Palaeologus and crown his son Matthew as co-emperor, but he did not succeed.

Medieval depiction of John V Palaeologus

By 1350, the Ottomans were involved directly in European affairs, including fighting with Genoa and Venice over control of trade on the Black Sea. The Ottomans took the side of Genoa, which in return offered them boats to ferry their people across the Bosporus. An unwitting John Cantacuzenus assisted Orhan's expansion efforts, and before long the Ottomans under Orhan had settled in Thrace and acquired their first stronghold in the Balkans. By the time Orhan died in 1362 and left control of the Ottomans to his son Murad, the Ottomans controlled much of southern Thrace, the frontier line was significantly further west than it had begun, and the eastern side of the empire extended as far as Ankara because they had captured the domains of a rival Turk dynasty.

Meanwhile, John Cantacuzenus continued to lose popularity among his Byzantine citizens until he was finally was forced to retire to a monastery, but the emperor's unpopularity was not a reflection of his commitment to the empire. As John Julius Norwich writes, "few emperors worked harder for the imperial good; few possessed less personal ambition." He explains that for John Cantacuzenus, "the greatest burden was the moral and financial bankruptcy of the empire itself. The treasury was empty; the Byzantines themselves had lost heart."

When Stephen Dushan died in 1355, his Serbian empire dissolved, but the Ottomans were spreading. John V Palaeologus, who now ruled the Byzantine Empire uncontested, became so desperate for allies that he traveled to Hungary to seek help from King Louis the Great. It was unprecedented for an emperor to leave the empire except as the head of the army, but Louis, hated schismatics (members of Christian orders other than his own - in this case, hating the Byzantines' Orthodoxy in comparison to his Catholicism). John V Palaeologus was captured by the Bulgars, and though he was saved by his cousin Amadeus VI, count of Savoy, the Byzantine emperor was only aided in being returned to the throne if he agreed to submit to Amadeus' agenda: a church union. John V Palaeologus consented on a personal submission to Rome, but stated that, as far as the Byzantine people were concerned, a "union could not be imposed from above; the Emperor had no authority over the souls of his subjects." He suggested that their differences could be settled by having an ecumenical council, in which all the Christian nations would be welcome and unified, but Rome was not willing. John V Palaeologus nevertheless kept his promise of submission, and in return, he was invited to Venice, only to be detained as a debtor and essentially made a prisoner.

On September 26, 1371, the Turks destroyed the Serbian army, and with the Turks in control of Serbia and Bulgaria, Byzantium was effectively cut off from the west. John V Palaeologus hoped to keep the potential damage in check by joining forces with Sultan Murad, to the extent that John and his heir apparent, Manuel, offered increased tributes, additional military assistance, and the city of Philadelphia (the last Byzantine outpost in Asia Minor) in exchange for reinstatement as Byzantine emperor. Nonetheless, by 1381, the Byzantine Empire could no longer faithfully be called an empire but rather, in the words of John Julius Norwich, "four small states ruled by four so-called emperors and a despot". Shortly thereafter, these emperors became vassals of the Turks.

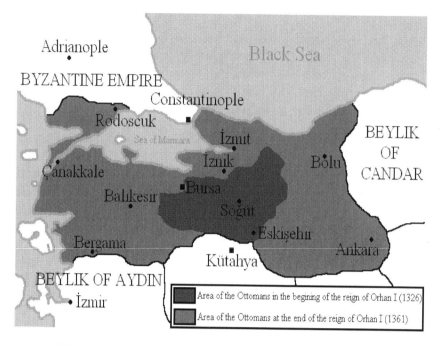

The spread of the Ottoman Empire under Orhan in the 14th century

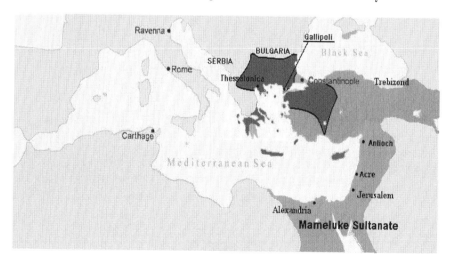

The Byzantine Empire (in purple) in 1389

In June 1389, Sultan Murad invaded Serbia and completely defeated the Serbians, but one of the captured Boyars managed to plunge a dagger twice into the Sultan's heart and kill him near the town of Pristina. Soon after, the Serbian sovereign Lazar was brought to an Ottoman tent and decapitated. The Ottomans were victorious, but both sovereigns were dead. When the news of the murder first spread to Europe, it was received as great news for Christendom, but when the news of Serbia's defeat spread, they realized the Ottoman armies were unconquerable by anything less than a concerted Crusade. At that point, such a crusade was impossible with the resources they had.

Murad was succeeded by his son Bayezid, and the Ottoman Empire that Bayezid inherited included an occupied Serbia. The succession of Bayezid is an opportunity to remember that the Ottomans were one of many Turkish groups in Asia Minor, and that their expansion was not unopposed by other Muslims. Bayezid's succession emboldened an anti-Ottoman alliance led by his very own brother-in-law, Alaeddin Bey of Karaman. When the Ottomans pushed southward, hoping to control trade routes to the Mediterranean, Alaeddin Bey himself initiated hostilities, attempting to prevent the Ottomans' expansionist goals.

Together with the Ottomans' neighboring vassals, Stephen Lazarevic of Serbia and Manuel II Palaeologus of Byzantium, Bayezid conquered some of the last few territories in Anatolia that had held out from Ottoman control. Though he obliged to his duties to Bayezid, Manuel II wrote the following letter on his campaign, conveying his feelings about the Ottoman leader and his expansion: "Certainly the Romans had a name for the small plain where we are now when they lived and ruled here...There are many cities here, but they lack what constitutes the true splendor of a city...that is, human beings. Most now lie in ruins...not even the names have survived...I cannot tell you exactly where we are...It is hard to bear all this...the scarcity of supplies, the severity of winter and the sickness which has struck down many of our men...[have] greatly depressed me...it is unbearable...to be unable to see anything, hear anything, do anything during all this time which could somehow...lift our spirit. This terribly oppressive time makes no concession to us who regard it of prime importance to remain aloof from and to have absolutely nothing to do with what we are now involved in or anything connected with it, for we are not educated for this sort of thing, nor accustomed to enjoy it, nor is it in our nature. The blame lies with the present state of affairs, not to mention the individual [Bayezid] whose fault they are."

The Byzantines were also ordered by Bayezid to be obedient during the Ottoman siege of Philadelphia, essentially forcing the Byzantines to be instrumental in their own decline. No doubt suffering from humiliation, John V Palaeologus died on February 16, 1391, but while he was now fully in charge of the Byzantine Empire, Manuel II was nothing more than a vassal. That year, he was summoned to help another Ottoman campaign to seize the Black Sea and thus control important trade and military routes and territories.

Medieval depiction of Manuel II

Sultan Bayezid I

Chapter 3: Bayezid's Siege of Constantinople

In 1393, Sultan Bayezid called his principal Christian vassals to his camp at Serres and Manuel obliged. Though some feared he would slay them all, he simply reprimanded them for poor governance of their territories and sent them on their way. However, the next time Bayezid summoned his vassals, Manuel refused. Bayezid interpreted his defiance as war, and indeed, Manuel had only taken the risk because he believed in the impregnability of Constantinople. He also knew that Bayezid had no navy, but to help his cause, Manuel reached out to other Christian empires for assistance. Sigismund of Hungary made a general appeal to the princes of Christendom, and this time, sensing how dire the circumstances of the Byzantine Empire were, they responded. Even the rival popes, Boniface IX in Rome and Benedict XIII in Avignon, responded.

Manuel did have good reasons to believe in Constantinople's ability to defend itself. At the end of the 14th century, Constantinople was the most impregnable city in the world, surrounded entirely by a complex and gigantic system of walls. The city's location on a triangular spit of land, guarded by the Bosporus Straits on one side and the Sea of Marmara on another, meant only one side could be approached by land. On the water-facing sides, the city had high sea walls and promontories from which the Byzantines could bombard any ships approaching the city. On the only land side, the city boasted the famous Theodosian Walls, which were constructed in the

5th century and were fortified by alternating moats with stone walls. The innermost wall stood 90 feet high and was more than 30 feet thick. These walls had protected Constantinople from siege by the Avars, Arabs, Rus' and Bulgars.

Even if insurgents were able to get beyond the walls, the Byzantines had a secret weapon called Byzantine Fire or Greek Fire, a burning substance launched from catapults that splashed when landed and stuck to flesh. It could not be doused with water, so it was especially useful to the Byzantines in naval battles because it could keep burning on water. The makeup of this mysterious substance remains a matter of debate, but suggestions include naptha, quicklime, sulfur, niter, and pine resin. Historian Tamim Ansary has labeled it "some primitive form of napalm."

A restored section of Constantinople's walls.

That spring, Bayezid embarked on his first attempt at a siege of Constantinople, and his first step in conducting a siege was to build a fortress a little more than 3 miles up the Bosporus from Constantinople. The castle was on the Asian side of the river at its narrowest point and was named Güzelcehisar ("Beauteous Castle"), and today it is called Anadolu Hisarı. The castle was finished by 1397.

While constructing a castle that would be integral to his siege of Constantinople, Bayezid tried to threaten Hungary, his most dangerous enemy in the Balkans, by seizing Macedonia in 1395 and then the city of Nikopol, giving the Ottomans control of the Balkans south of the Danube. From Nikopol, he sent his men into Hungary for the first time, and they raided far and wide. Alaeddin Bey, the Sultan's brother-in-law, made it known that he was not impressed by Bayezid's forceful expansion, but he paid for this pride with his life, and afterwards Bayezid claimed the Karamanid emirate for himself.

Constantinople's walls had kept many foreign invaders out, and it continued to hold out against Bayezid as Manuel sought help from Europe. In 1399, Charles VI of France sent 12,000 gold francs and a force of 1,200 men, led by the greatest French soldier of the day, Jean le Maingre, Marshal Boucicault. Boucicault managed to get through the Ottoman blockade and reach Constantinople in September, but he quickly realized that any effective army would have to be organized on a far larger scale than what was available between his men and Manuel's. Jean le Maingre insisted that the emperor himself go to Paris and plead his cause before the French king. Manuel agreed and was fêted all along the way by Christian leaders who newly supported him and viewed him as the defender of Christendom. When he arrived in Paris, an entire wing of the Louvre had been redecorated for him, but King Charles still refused to consider a full-scale international Crusade on behalf of the beleaguered Byzantines.

Contemporary painting of Charles VI of France

Chapter 4: Mehmed I and Murad II

Manuel stayed in Europe, traveling to appeal to England's King Henry IV, the kings of Aragon and Portugal, the Pope and Antipope. Though they received him warmly, he failed to generate the scale of support he desired, and the money collected for Manuel around England allegedly disappeared. This left Manuel in low spirits until Seigneur Jean de Chateaumorand, who Bouricault had left in charge of Constantinople, arrived with the news that the Mongols under Tamerlane had destroyed the Ottoman army and Bayezid had been taken prisoner. Tamerlane, known as the most ruthless and bloodthirsty of the Mongols, saw himself and his army as the descendents of Genghis Khan, while the Ottomans saw themselves as the heirs of the Sejluk state. After Bayezid's death at the hands of Tamerlane, he became revered as a tragic figure, as Ottoman historians passed down a legend of Tamerlane forcing him to sit in an iron cage as they crossed Anatolia, but the more likely story is that Bayezid committed suicide shortly after being taken prisoner.

Bayezid's death initiated a decade of friction between his sons, all vying for the prize of being Sultan, because Turks had no law of primogeniture (right of succession to the firstborn son). Prince Süleyman, the oldest of Bayezid's sons, took quick actions to prevent his Balkan vassals

(Byzantine, Serbian, and Latin) from taking advantage of the disintegration of the Ottoman regime, and he also quickly started negotiations in order to prevent them from exercising historical claims to territories within his weakened realm. In 1403, however, after he had been unable to regain power, Süleyman was forced to make previously unthinkable territorial concessions. In the Treaty of 1403, Süleyman released Byzantine vassalage, returned Thessalonica to Byzantine control, released Byzantine prisoners, and agreed that Turkish vessels would no longer enter Constantinople's harbor without permission. In essence, Manuel had found himself in a much better position while overseas.

After Bayezid's death, his son Mehmed retired to his base in north-central Anatolia, only to re-emerge when Tamerlane returned eastward in 1403, but for the next few years, Süleyman ruled with stability after his treaty with the Byzantine Empire. He expanded his reign to include Bursa and Ankara in 1404, and achieved high enough status that some historians consider him to have been a sultan, Süleyman I.

However, in 1411, Süleyman's younger brother Musa captured Adrianople, after which Süleyman was taken prisoner and instantly strangled. The field of contestants for succession to the Ottoman throne was now reduced to Mehmed and Musa, but for now, Musa was the more powerful brother. Almost as quickly as he put his brother to death, Musa abrogated the Treaty of 1403 and declared his brother's various concessions null and void.

Manuel had been pleased with the instability that the brothers' competition brought on and did his best to prolong it, but in 1411, Musa tried to lay siege to Constantinople because Süleyman's son Orhan had taken refuge there, and Musa was worried that he would pose a threat. Desperate for help in staving off Musa, the Byzantine emperor dispatched an embassy to Mehmed's court at Brusa. An alliance with Manuel seemed a small price to pay for Mehmed, so he led a huge army against Musa and defeated him at Camurlu in Serbia on July 5, 1413. Musa was strangled in the battle, and with that, the succession went to Mehmed, now called Sultan Mehmed I.

A medieval depiction of Mehmed I

Mehmed was so grateful to be the unopposed leader of the Ottomans that he wrote the following letter to Manuel: "Go and say to my father the emperor of the Romans that from this day forth I am and shall be his subject, as a son to his father. Let him but command me to do his bidding, and I shall with the greatest pleasure execute his wishes as his servant." As long as they were both alive, there was no change in the friendly status quo between Mehmed and Manuel.

Mehmed's first goal was winning the allegiance of the Anatolian communities who had gained independence since Tamerlane's victory. He met with resistance from Karaman and Cüneyd (emir of Aydın), but he eventually captured Cüneyd's territory and appointed Cüneyd the governor of Nikopol, in keeping with the tradition of Ottoman governance to appoint former rebels to administrative posts in hopes of keeping them content and docile. Because of Mehmed's successes, Manuel's position was further weakened, even as the two remained outwardly friendly.

The Ottomans met opposition of a new kind in 1416 with the rise of several cult-like charismatic figures, most notably Sheikh Bedreddin, a member of a religious hierarchy who was born of mixed Christian-Muslim heritage and preached "oneness of being", the idea that there was no difference between religions and prophets. He was so captivating that he successfully brought about a revolt in Rumeli, but the revolt was short lived, and Mehmed's men apprehended and executed him. The story of Sheikh Bedreddin later inspired Turkish poet Nazim Hıkmet in his anti-fascist struggle in the 1930's, and Bedreddin was the topic of Hıkmet's epic poem *The Epic of Sheikh Bedreddin.*

When Mehmed died suddenly in a horse accident in 1421, his successor was his son, Sultan Murad II. As he came to power, Murad had to fight off two "false Mustafas" who claimed the right to the throne on the grounds that they were Mehmed's lost brother Mustafa. The first of the two was beaten in battle, and the second was strangled on the grounds that no sacrifice was too great for the maintenance of the public order.

Murad II

Sultan Murad II continued his father's efforts to rebuild the Ottoman state, and though pesky Karaman remained independent, Murad consolidated his rule. This also meant the period of respite for the Byzantines came to an end. A holy man foretold to Murad II that Constantinople would fall on August 24, so Murad waited all summer until that date to make an attack on the city. Fortunately for the Byzantines, the city's defenses again held, and rightly sensing that Murad II was not a leader who was willing to work with him, the Byzantine emperor - now very old - conspired to put the Sultan's youngest son, Mustafa, on the Ottoman throne. Shortly thereafter, however, Manuel was bedridden by a stroke. He resigned from the throne, became a monk, and died in July of 1425.

Upon Manuel's death, John VIII Palaeologus became the sole leader of the Byzantines, but by this time, Constantinople was a dismal place. It had no more than 50,000 inhabitants, was economically desperate, suffering from famine, and had a devalued economy. Every day saw a further decrease in manpower for the defense of the city's land walls, and the situation was so ugly that four of Manuel's sons had chosen to flee the city altogether and head for the Despotate of the Morea (a province of the empire that included most of southern Greece's Peloponnesian peninsula) because they believed the despotate was even more protected and defensible than the walled city.

A medieval painting of John VIII Palaeologus

From 1424-1426, Murad attacked his vassal states of Wallachia and Serbia to prevent them from joining forces with Hungary and Venice, and the Ottomans proceeded to engage in a land-grabbing game of chicken against Hungary. It ended with a treaty in 1428, but by then the frontier lines of the two empires were closer than they had ever been. After that, a war between Venice and the Ottomans was declared in 1429. The city fell to Murad in 1430, but with its capture Murad allowed a treaty that prevented looting, restored its inhabitants, began reconstruction efforts, and converted only two of the city's churches to mosques - a sign of the city's still small Muslim population.

With those conquests behind him, the power struggle in the Balkans became the Sultan's priority. Before the Ottomans' treaty with Hungary had even expired, the empire began movement into Albania. However, the empire's focus in the Balkans meant that the emir of Karaman, Ibrahim Bey, saw an opportunity to attack certain territories in Anatolia, but his movements merely led to more territorial gains for the Ottomans, even though they still lacked the resources to fully subjugate Karaman. The Balkans occupied Murad for the remainder of his reign; his next success was that the key stronghold of Belgrade succumbed in 1440 after a six-month siege.

While he was active in the Balkans, Murad also stayed busy fighting the Byzantines. Recommencing his efforts to finally subdue Constantinople, Murad captured Thessalonica, the second largest city in the Byzantine Empire, in a matter of hours. Now sensing dire straits, Pope Martin V summoned a council of the church to meet at Basel in 1431, and to John VIII Palaeologus, this seemed like a ray of hope because the Byzantines suddenly had the opportunity to appeal to Christian nations for help. The council got off to a bad start, distracted by competition between the emperor and the pope, but by the end of the meeting, the church was theoretically reunited in 1439, undoing its 375-year-old schism (at least on paper). Even still, the Orthodox establishment was divided about whether to support the union, and Central Europe remained at odds with the Latins of the Mediterranean, but this meant that the pope would raise his promised crusade against Byzantium's enemies.

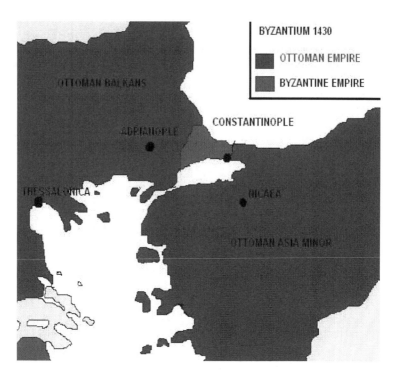

The extent of the Byzantine and Ottoman Empires in 1430

Hungarians formed the bulk of the crusade, and an additional fleet was provided by the Venetians, the Duke of Burgundy, and the Pope. These forces set off in the summer of 1443. That December, Sofia surrendered, and several smaller subsequent victories were enough to alarm the Sultan. The Sultan subsequently offered a truce, and when the Pope heard about the truce, he communicated to the Hungarian King Ladislas that he was no longer obligated to assist the Byzantines. At the time, Ladislas was ready to go and was expecting the fleet to come to Hungary so that they could push forward, but the fleet was busy fighting the Ottomans, preventing Ladislas from crossing the Bosporus.

Around the same time Central Europe signed the 10-year truce with Murad in 1444, the sultan summoned his son Mehmed to Edirne, the Ottoman capital, and announced plans to give up the throne. His motive remains unknown and is still a matter of speculation among historians. Perhaps he was tired out from 20 years of rule, or perhaps he was saddened by the recent death of his older brother, but whatever the case, his abdication and passing of the throne to his 12 year old son was taken by his competitors as a sign of weakness to be exploited. Ironically, Mehmed II was the son of a slave girl from a Turkish harem and was thus probably Christian, given that most women in Turkish harems were Christian girls from the Caucasus.

Mehmed II

Absolved by the Pope of their duties to the oath, the Hungarian and Polish leaders swore fake oaths at the signing of the truce, but shortly after, crusading Hungarians crossed the Danube and marched to the Black Sea coast. Only George Brankovic of Serbia declined to join, because Murad had promised Serbia independence. As they advanced, there was a great sense of fear in Edirne. Because Mehmed was so young, Murad had put his trusted vezir, Çandarlı Halil Pasha, in charge of overseeing him. The Çandarlı family had been with the Ottomans as first ministers since the reign of Murad I, but there were other "professional Ottomans" who were jealous of Çandarlı Halil Pasha's pre-eminent position and wanted something more than the stable state governing Anatolia and Rumeli toward which Murad had been directing the empire.

Çandarlı Halil Pasha was reluctant to allow the enthusiastic young Sultan to lead an army against the crusaders, and alarmed at the civil unrest in Edirne, he felt he had only one choice: to call back Murad. Murad didn't enter the city but led his army directly against the Hungarians. During the fighting, King Ladislas was killed, and the Hungarian troops fled. By November 1444, the crusaders had been completely crushed, putting an end to the crusade.

This was a great humiliation for John VIII Palaeologus, who died two weeks later. Since he died childless, envoys decided that his successor would be his brother Constantine. However, Constantine XI Dragases could never be formally crowned because since the council of Florence in 1439, the Orthodox Church had been in schism, conflicted between the pro-union and anti-union sides.

After beating back the crusaders, Murad left power again, only to be called out of retirement a second time to deal with an insurrection caused by Mehmed debasing the Ottoman currency by more than 10%, which had put pressure on salaried state employees whose paychecks were suddenly worth less than before. However, upon Murad's return, many believed the Ottoman state had two sultans, with Mehmed ruling Rumeli and Murad ruling Anatolia. Ultimately, the protestors, demanding that Mehmed be removed from power, got their way; Mehmed would be out of power until Murad's death in 1451.

Chapter 5: The Fall of Constantinople

From the moment Mehmed finally succeeded to the Ottoman throne for good in 1451, he took no chance to be vulnerable. For instance, when Murad's widow arrived to congratulate him on his succession, Mehmed received her warmly, but when she returned to her harem she found that her infant son had been drowned in the bath.

That same year, Mehmed moved to secure his borders. He renewed his treaty with Brankovic, leader of Serbia, and created a three-year treaty with Hunyadi, regent of Hungary. He also confirmed a treaty with Venice that his father had made in 1446. All of this would also help further his designs on Constantinople, which the Ottomans had ample reason for coveting. Control of the Bosporus would be extremely advantageous, and control of the Byzantine territory would bring large financial benefits in the form of taxation to the Ottomans. The Ottomans even described the city as their "red apple", an expression for their ultimate aspiration.

Mehmed's attack would be the 13th attempt at conquest against Constantinople, and he intended to do it right. In 1451, he began to build a fortress on the Bosporus at the place where the channel was at its narrowest, opposite Sultan Bayezid's Anadolu Hisar castle. Between the two castles, the Ottomans now had complete control of the Bosporus, which provided them with an ideal base from which to attack Constantinople from the northeast. Emperor Constantine sent embassies to speak with the Ottomans, but they were executed on the spot. Every passing ship was inspected, and when one Venetian ship disobeyed, everyone was killed.

In 1453, Mehmed told his advisors that his empire was not safe as long as Constantinople remained in Christian hands. He began to gather an army in Thrace, and every Ottoman regiment, along with hordes of mercenaries, were recruited; all in all, there were 80,000 regular troops and 20,000 *bashi-bazouks* ("others"), though some historians estimate there were as many as 160,000 troops. Furthermore, the year before, a German engineer called Urban had offered to build the Ottomans a cannon that would blast any walls, so the Ottomans paid for and received the weapon three months later. They then demanded one twice the size and received it in January 1453. It was 27 feet long and 8 inches thick, with a muzzle that was 2.5 feet across, making it capable of shooting a ball some 1,300 pounds a distance of over a mile. 200 men helped the cannon make its journey south to the outside of Constantinople's walls, and their manpower was also needed for smoothing out the road and reinforcing bridges.

Fausto Zorano's painting, *Mehmet II conquering Constantinople*

Orthodox Easter 1453 was on the 1st of April, and on April 5th, Mehmed pitched a tent and sent a message to Constantine - one required under Islamic law - offering to spare all subjects in return for immediate surrender. He received no reply, so the cannon opened fire the next day. The people of Constantinople were not surprised, as they had worked in previous months on their city's defenses, but they were sorely lacking in resources. At their disposal, they had only eight Venetian vessels, five Genoese, and one vessel each from Ancona, Catalonia, and Provence. From the Byzantine Empire's own navy, there were only 10 vessels, meaning they only had 26 ships total. In terms of manpower, there were only 4,983 able-bodied Greeks and 2,000 foreigners, much too few to stand guard along 14 miles of wall, let alone face the 100,000 strong Ottoman army.

The siege lines, with the Ottomans in green and the Byzantines in red.

Nonetheless, all the defenders were in their places when the firing started. The emperor and Giovanni Giustiniani, the Genoese captain, were in command of the most vulnerable section, the area of the wall that crossed the valley of the little river Lycus about a mile from the northern end. The sea walls were less thoroughly manned than the land walls, but their garrisons also served as lookouts, reporting on the movements of the Turkish ships.

Despite these defenses, the Sultan was subjecting the land walls to a bombardment unprecedented in the history of siege warfare. By the evening of that first day, Mehmed II and the Ottoman troops had pulverized a section near the Charisius Gate, after which his soldiers tried to smash their way through, but it held. They went back to their camp at nightfall, and the Byzantines rebuilt it overnight.

Mehmed decided to hold his fire until he could bring reinforcements, and the bombardment resumed on April 11, continuing 48 more days uninterrupted. The larger cannon could only be fired once every two or three hours, but the damage was enormous, and within a week, the outer wall across the Lycus had collapsed in several places. The Byzantines worked ceaselessly to repair it, but the damage continued.

On April 20, ships from Genoa arrived off the Hellespont. Because Sultan Mehmed was determined to amass the strongest possible naval force outside Constantinople, he had left those straits unguarded, so the arriving ships were able to enter into the Marmara unhindered. As they arrived, the Sultan rode around the head of the Golden Horn to give the order personally to his admiral, Süleyman Baltoglu, that they were absolutely not to be allowed to reach the city. Baltoglu prepared to attack, but there was a strong southerly breeze, and his ships were unmanageable against the heavy swell. His overwhelmed captains were virtually defenseless against the deluge of arrows and javelins that greeted any approach, so they were forced to stand by as the ships sailed serenely toward the Golden Horn. When the wind dropped, Baltoglu gave the order to ram the Genoese ships and board them, but Turkish ships rode low in the water, so even when they successfully rammed the other vehicle, climbing into it was impossible. The Genoese sailors were also equipped with large axes and used them to take off the hands and heads of any who wished to enter. Ultimately, the Genoese captains lashed their ships together and were able to move toward the Horn as a giant floating fortress; a few hours later, in the middle of the night, they entered the city.

Sultan Mehmed II had watched every moment of the battle from land and was so furious with its outcome that he ordered Baltoglu's execution. The admiral avoided death after his subordinates testified to his courage, but he was nevertheless sent packing. The Sultan next set his sights on the Golden Horn. He had already put his engineers to work on a road running behind Galata, from the Marmara shore, over the hill near what is now Taksim Square, and down into the Horn itself. The engineers and laborers had cast iron wheels and metal tracks, and the carpenters were hard at work building wooden cradles that could hold the keels of moderate-sized vessels. It was a remarkable undertaking, and on Sunday, April 22, the Genoese colony in Galata watched with astonishment as 70 Turkish ships were hauled in by teams of oxen over the 200 foot hill and lowered into the Horn.

Fausto Zorano's painting, *Mehmed II at the siege of Constantinople*. This one depicts Ottoman troops transporting their fleet overland to the Golden Horn.

The Byzantines could not believe what was happening, and they no longer had a secure harbor, which also meant that they now had three and a half more miles of sea wall to defend, including the section breached by the Crusaders in 1204. Byzantine attempts to attack the Ottoman navy failed, while initial frontal assaults by the Ottomans also failed. Near the end of April, the defenders ostentatiously beheaded hundreds of Ottomans atop the walls as a sign for the invading army, but they would not be deterred. A Venetian in Constantinople at the time wrote in his diary, "They found the Turks coming right up under the walls and seeking battle, particularly the Janissaries...and when one or two of them were killed, at once more Turks came and took away the dead ones...without caring how near they came to the city walls. Our men shot at them with guns and crossbows, aiming at the Turk who was carrying away his dead countryman, and both of them would fall to the ground dead, and then there came other Turks and took them away, none fearing death, but being willing to let ten of themselves be killed rather than suffer the shame of leaving a single Turkish corpse by the walls."

Medieval depictions of the siege.

By the beginning of May, Constantine knew they would not hold out much longer; they were running out of food, and his troops were taking more and more time off of defending the city in order to find food for their families. His last faint hope was a promised Venetian relief mission, but he did not know whether it was actually on its way, what it held, or how big it was. He also did not know when it would come or how it would get through the Golden Horn, now that the Ottomans controlled it. He felt that his fate lay in the answers to these questions, so before midnight on May 3, a Venetian ship flying the Turkish flag and carrying a crew of 12 dressed in Turkish disguise slipped out.

Meanwhile, the Ottomans had given up on frontal attacks and were trying more traditional siege tactics, including tunneling under the walls to plant mines, not to mention the constant bombardment. The Byzantines dug counter-mines to locate and stop the Turkish tunnels, and they succeeded in destroying several Turkish attempts underground. Growing impatient, Mehmed sent a letter to Constantine on May 21 offering to let the people inside survive if they surrendered, and also letting Constantine head to the Peloponnese, which would be virtually the only remaining Byzantine possession. Constantine was willing to assent to the conditions, but not for the price of Constantinople, replying, "Giving you though the city depends neither on me nor on anyone else among its inhabitants; as we have all decided to die with our own free will and we shall not consider our lives."

However, two days later, when the secret Byzantine ship returned on May 23rd, its captain reported that they had combed the Aegean for weeks but had seen no trace of the promised Venetian relief expedition. Historian John Julius Norwich described the scene: "and so they had returned, knowing full well that they were unlikely to leave the city alive. Constantine thanked each one personally, his voice choked with tears."

There were also omens, or at least so they were interpreted by the Byzantines. On May 22 there was a lunar eclipse, and days later, as the holiest icon of the Virgin was being carried through the streets as an appeal to her intercession, it slipped from its platform. The morning after that, the city was shrouded in fog, which was unheard of at the end of May, and that same night the dome of St. Sophia was suffused with an unearthly red glow from the base to the summit, something that was even disturbing to Mehmed. His astrologers assured him that it was a sign that the building would soon be illuminated by the True Faith, and the Byzantines took it as a sign that the Spirit of God had deserted their city. Constantine's ministers begged him to leave the capital while there was still time and lead the empire from the Morea until he could recover the city. He fainted just as they spoke this suggestion; but when he recovered, he was determined as ever to not leave his people.

Meanwhile, the Sultan held a council of war on May 26, where he declared that the siege had continued long enough and that the time had come for a final assault. He announced that the following day would be filled with preparations, and the one after with rest and prayer, but they would begin the attack the morning of May 29, and they made no effort to conceal their plans from the Byzantines. They prepared for the next 36 hours without interruption, even lighting huge flares at night to help the soldiers with their labors. Then, at dawn on the 28th, they ceased. Mehmed set off on a day-long tour to inspect their preparations, finishing late in the evening and exhausted.

Inside the city, work on the city walls continued, but the people also gathered for one last collective appeal to God. Bells pealed, and the most sacred icons and precious relics were carried out to join a long spontaneous procession passing through the streets and along the whole length of the walls. They paused for special prayers where they expected the Ottoman artillery to concentrate particularly heavily. When the procession finished, the Emperor summoned his commanders and told his Greek subjects that there were four causes worth sacrificing one's life: his faith, his country, his family, and his sovereign. The Emperor told them they must be prepared to give their lives for all four tomorrow, and that he was prepared to sacrifice his own life. Next, he turned to the Italians and thanked them for their service. He told them that they and the Greeks were now one people, and that with God's help they would be victorious.

At dusk on the 28th, people from all over the city made their way to the Church of Holy

Wisdom - St. Sophia, the spiritual center of Byzantium - for the last service of vespers ever to be held in it. Virtually every man, woman and child who was not on duty that evening gathered in the Hagia Sophia to take the Eucharist and pray for deliverance. The Emperor arrived and asked for forgiveness for his sins from every bishop present, both Catholic and Orthodox, and then took communion. Later, after all the candles were out and the church was entirely dark, he spent time in prayer before returning home for a last farewell to his household. Around midnight, he rode the length of the land walls to assure himself that everything was ready.

Picture of the Hagia Sophia taken by Arild Vågen

Mehmed gave his signal at 1:30 in the morning on the 29th, and suddenly the silence was shattered. The Turks made their advance known with blasts of trumpets, hammering of drums, and bloodcurdling war cries. The Byzantine church bells pealed in response. The final battle had begun.

Mehmed knew that to succeed, he could not allow the Byzantines any rest. He first sent forward his mercenary soldiers, the *bashi-bazouks*, who were poorly armed and poorly trained, but they commanded some terrifying initial force. They flung themselves against the walls for two hours. Then, shortly before four in the morning, Mehmed called for the second wave of the attack, made by several regiments of Anatolian Turks who were significantly better trained and disciplined. They nearly forced entry, but the defenders - led by the Emperor himself - closed around them, killed many, and forced them back.

Mehmed determined that victory must be won not by the Anatolians but by his very own elite regiment of Janissaries. He next sent them into battle, offering the Byzantines no time to rest. The Ottoman troops advanced swiftly across the plain, hurling themselves at the stockades and hacking away at the supports. They also put up scaling-ladders to climb the walls. Instead of attempting to use them, however, these Janissaries had the opportunity to alternate with a fourth round of troops and rest while they waited for their next turn. The defenders, short-handed and exhausted, had no opportunity. They could not last much longer, but the walls still hadn't given way.

As if the defenders didn't have enough problems, they were struck with bad luck literally when shortly after dawn, Giovanni Giustiniani, the Genoese general who had been guarding the wall's weakest point with the emperor, was struck by lightning. In excruciating pain, he was carried to a Genoese ship in the harbor, but before the gate could be relocked, Mehmed saw the opening and sent in another wave of Janissaries. They forced the Greeks to retreat to the inner wall, and once they were caught between the two rows of walls, they were trapped and highly vulnerable. Many were slaughtered in place.

A short distance to the north, both sides could see a Turkish flag now flying over a tower. An hour before the slaughter between the fortifications, a group of Turkish mercenaries had found a small door, half-hidden at the foot of a tower, that was unlocked. It was a sally-port through which the Genoese had executed several effective raids on the Turkish camp, but now the *bashi-bazouks* mercenaries managed to force it open and make their way to the top of the tower. They hoisted their flag, left the door open for others to follow, and Turkish regiments poured in through all the open breaches. Emperor Constantine plunged right into the fray and was never seen again.

Theophilos Hatzimihail's depiction of fighting inside Constantinople. Constantine is depicted on the white horse.

By early morning, there were scarcely any living defenders. All the surviving Greeks had raced home to try to protect their families from the Ottomans' raping and pillaging, the Venetians were racing to the harbor, and the Genoese were trusting in the relative security of Galata. The Genoese found the Horn by and large quiet, while the Venetians had no trouble getting out of the harbor, into the Marmara, and out to the open sea.

As was often the custom in the Middle Ages, the Ottomans were ruthless in their ransacking. By noon, the streets were full of running blood, women and children were raped or stabbed, and churches, icons, and books were destroyed. The Empire's holiest icon, the virgin Hodegetria, was hacked into four pieces and destroyed. One writer said that blood flowed in the city "like rainwater in the gutters after a sudden storm", and that the bodies of both Turks and Byzantines floated in the sea "like melons along a canal".

The worst massacre was at the Hagia Sophia, where services were underway when the Turks began attempting to raze the church. The Christians shut the great bronze doors, but the Turks smashed their way in. The congregation was all either massacred on the spot or carted away to a Turkish prison camp. The priests tried to continue with mass until they were killed at the altar. Some Christians believe that a few of them managed to grab the patens and chalices and disappear in to the southern wall of the sanctuary, to wait until the city became a Christian city again, at which time they would resume the service right where it was left off.

Sultan Mehmed had promised his soldiers the traditional three days of looting, but by evening there was nothing left, and he called it off to little protest.

The historian and administrator Tursun Bey provided the sole detailed contemporary account of the siege in the Ottoman language:

> "Once the cloud of smoke of Greek fire and the soul of the Fire-worshipping Prince had descended over the castle 'as though a shadow,' the import was manifest: the devout Sultan of good fortune had, as it were, 'suspended the mountain' over this people of polytheism and destruction like the Lord God himself. Thus, both from within and without, [the shot of] the cannons and muskets and falconets and small arrows and arrows and crossbows spewed and flung out a profusion of drops of Pharaonic-seeming perspiration as in the rains of April - like a messenger of the prayers of the righteous - and a veritable precipitation and downpouring of calamities from the heavens as decreed by God. And, from the furthest reaches below to the top-most parts, and from the upper heights down to ground level, hand-to-hand combat and charging was being joined with a clashing and plunging of arms and hooked pikes and halberds in the breaches amidst the ruin wrought by the cannon.

> On the outside the Champions of Islam and on the inside the wayward ones,

> pike to pike in true combat, hand-to-hand;

> Now advancing now feinting, guns [firing] and arms drawn,

> Countless heads were severed from their trunks;

> Expelling the smoke of the Greek fire, a veritable cloud

> of sparks was rained on the Champions of Islam by the infidels;

> Ramming into the castle walls, the trenches in this manner,

> They set off the Greek fire, the enemies;

> [In turn] they presented to the bastion their hooked pikes,

> Drawn, they were knocking to the ground the engaged warriors,

> As if struck in the deepest bedrock by the digging of a tunnel

It seemed that in places the castle had been pierced from below.

By the early part of the forenoon, the frenzy of the fiery tumult and the dust of strife had died away."

Fausto Zorano's painting, *Mehmed II, Entering to Constantinople*

George Sphrantzes, who was in Constantinople when it fell, wrote about the aftermath: "On the third day after the fall of our city, the Sultan celebrated his victory with a great, joyful triumph. He issued a proclamation: the citizens of all ages who had managed to escape detection were to leave their hiding places throughout the city and come out into the open, as they were remain free and no question would be asked. He further declared the restoration of houses and property to those who had abandoned our city before the siege, if they returned home, they would be treated according to their rank and religion, as if nothing had changed."

Perhaps most notably, after the siege was complete, Mehmed, Tursun Bey, the empire's chief ministers, imams, and the Janissaries rode to the Hagia Sophia. Mehmed picked up a handful of earth and sprinkled it over his turban as he entered as a gesture of humility, and as he approached the altar, he stopped one of the soldiers he saw hacking at the building's marble and informed him that looting did not apply to public buildings. He then commanded the senior imam to ascend to the altar and proclaim the name of Allah. With nothing more than the removal of Christian paraphernalia and their replacement with Muslim pulpits and minarets, the legendary Hagia Sophia became a mosque.

The simplicity of the transformation was at once delicate and brutal, as evidenced by the way it's referred to among the Western world and the Turks. In the Christian world, the events are known as "the Fall", but for the Ottomans of history and the Turks of today, it was and remains "the Conquest."

Bibliography

Ansary, Tamim. *Destiny Disrupted: A History of the World Through Islamic Eyes.* New York: Public Affairs, 2009.

Herrin, Judith. *Byzantium: The Surprising Life of a Medieval Empire.* Princeton: Princeton University Press, 2009.

Finkel, Caroline. *Osman's Dream: The Story of the Ottoman Empire 1300-1923.* New York: Perseus, 2005.

Imber, Colin. *The Ottoman Empire, 1300-1650.* London: Palgrave Macmillan, 2009.

Loomis, Louise Ropes. "The Fall of Constantinople Symbolically Considered." *Essays in Intellectual History.* New York: Harper and Brothers, 1929. 243-258.

Nicol, D.M. *The End of the Byzantine Empire.* Teaneck: Holmes & Meier, 1980.

Norwich, John Julius. *A Short History of Byzantium.* New York: Vintage, 1997.

Treadgold, Warren. *A History of the Byzantine State and Society.* Redwood City: Stanford University Press, 2007.

Made in the USA
San Bernardino, CA
09 August 2015